Breathing Arizona

A Journal

Breathing Arizona

A Journal

Stephen Bett

for Jeff!

Stef

Dec '14

Ekstasis Editions

© Stephen Bett 2014
Cover photo: Nolan Bett
Author photo: Katie Bett

Published in 2014 by:
Ekstasis Editions Canada Ltd.   Ekstasis Editions
Box 8474, Main Postal Outlet   Box 571
Victoria BC V8W 3S1   Banff AB T1L 1E3

LIBRARY AND ARCHIVES CANADA CATALOGUING IN PUBLICATION

Bett, Stephen, author
      Breathing Arizona : a journal / Stephen Bett.

Poems.
Issued in print and electronic formats.
ISBN 978-1-77171-031-2 (pbk.).--ISBN 9781771710411 (ebook)

      I. Title.

PS8553.E834J68 2014   C811'.54   C2014-902370-7
                                         C2014-903075-4

Canada Council   Conseil des Arts
for the Arts   du Canada

Ekstasis Editions acknowledges financial support for the publication of *Breath-
ing Arizona: A Journal* from the government of Canada through the Canada
Book Fund and the Canada Council for the Arts, and from the Province of
British Columbia through the Book Publishing Tax Credit.

Printed and bound in Canada

for Katie, whose breath brings love

Don't know why you had
to go thru hell to get
here

Hades, Inferno, *what-*
ever ...

Some one (or thing) must
have thought it would be
a *damned* fine
idea

For sure it wasn't any
fun   —drank & soaked
yourself every night
(worthless poison
tears)

No-one should suffer
like that is what you
told yourself
(completely
convinced)

That "you" was me
(undoubtedly)

*

Took nearly half a
year to dry out
the towel

That done, I swear
(stunned self)
a miracle
appeared,
woman from
the Arizona
desert

No tears in
your eyes

And no
mirage
(either)

Clear vision
that moves
miles in-
ward

*

If my dear Romanian
woman friend is
right & man is
chaser, woman
chooser
I've run several
marathons to
you by now

*

Another friend tells me
it *is* possible to
have a second
love supreme
tracking one's
life
(a kind of
exquisite
female
spirit
Trane)

It took hard fraught
love & a lifetime
to find each
other

God it took forever
& now there's one
more forever
between &
around
us,
love

*

Her new boyfriend's
a frickin' poet for
christ sake what
d' u make
of that

Probably speaks in
rhyme & shits
in limericks

What kind of
asshole would
do that
          & Canai-
jun too

Yah jes caint
tell with
some
guys
(huh?
… eh?)

Better bail
girl, quick

Before he's
got you
SOL &
over a
limp-
wrist
moon

*

Head-weary
(def-o, after
all this
horror
show)

But heart-up
again

Skip a few
beats for
you,
pictures
alive

I would
frame
you

Forever
in my
moving
eye

*

No defeatist thinking
pls, love

If this "doesn't work"

(for some dumb reason
prob. my fault not
try hard enough?
only guarantee,
blood in heart)

will I at least be
your friend
forever?

No, I already have
enough friends to
shake many sticks
at

               (& do—with regularity,
               they are too well
               beaten by now!)

This is strictly romantic
(a "plus")
I want only
to *love* you
"forever"
               (Period.)

Deep friendship
—this bonus,
A+ karmic
law that
follows

Will follow
               (sure —as faith
               itself)

Keep the faith
bro, sisters
(of long nites)
all we have left
by dawn

No permit to
let us down
again
        (no *per*-mit &
        no per-*mit*)

Going for broke
this time
        (& will not be
        broken —before
        or after mid-nite
        singes our eyes)

I have plenty desire
to burn into
your soul
desert woman
—eyes open &
on fire
        (re-purify the al-
        ready purified,
        woman alive,
        heart's own
        blood)

                *

A-muricano woman,
why did he spend
his life with his
country-women
—while you drew
breath in a
southern state
(of mind)

His own mother would
have chosen you
for him
(from this
continent of un-
finished &
inalienable
rights)

Be blessed
with that
right
choice
after
all

Unfurled truth of
sibling nations

Close watch alert
& a mother's
silence played
out this destiny
of histories

Her deepest wish
for the son
she grew …
you enter
her voice
here

Long after her
breath has
gone out

She thinks
of you
(& you
together)

Children of your
two solitudes
united &
reunited

In the only
freedom
possible
—for
love

*

My son is troubled
by love (mid-
twenties)

It takes a long
long time
to learn
where the
heart is
truly
at

And that it
takes a basic
precedence

Finally I got
the location
right

It is in my
chest &
reaches
out for
yours,
love

We bleed
for our
children
(or course)
& we never
stop bleed-
ing for
ourselves

We learn some
lessons   — &
others are
beyond us
still

They make us
bleed even
more

And make us
human to
each other

Such love
defines
you,
Katie
love

May I love
my son
like this ...

*

We will give this
time to breathe,
love

If it catches or
stumbles, let
it right
itself

By now this
will happen
on its own

The breath &
the feet will
be in sync

And the pro-
prioceptive
will dance

It is pro-
jective &
reaches
outward
& about

Like the man
said

And it's
coming
for you
(& for
us
too)

*

Where you at
girl (A-muricano
woman) ?

You are at
my heart,
flying
low
—just above
ground

Straight at
the vital
organ that
pumps
blood

In the
stream
of things,
so to
speak

And bless
you for
being
there
(here)

Stay as long
as you can
(or will)

Even for-
ever

It is up
to you
of course

But this
stream
can be
a river
for thee
& me

Open all the
way to the
western
sea

Carry us
both in
tow

Our final
ease &
release

*

I have kissed the top
of my son's head
a thousand times

& my daughter's cheek
(even more?)

I want so much to
kiss your fearless
closed eyes

& your smiling mouth
(hold your face silent
in my palms)

Human places in this
hard to locate world
I will touch only
with care
—feel strong for
doing so

*

It is your day
(today)
A-muricano
woman
—woman of
independence

Grabbed my
heart too
(way more
than a fourth)

Tugged it
(three quarters
at least)
south

I've always
been un-
comfortable
there
(we all
are here
a' boots)

Will do
this now
there is
a full
reason

*

Missed you today

This is an unhappy
world (I notice)

We can only make
it happy for
ourselves
(is true,
non?)

You are so close
to me now, only
two hours
away

I am about to
fall (from such
proximity)
—pls catch me
(on the way
down?)

Maybe fall a-
gainst or into
each other ?

Right there, on
the tarmac
by "arrivals"
(we have,
like,
arrived
…)

What else *is*
there, at
this point

It is all
to die for
we keep
telling
ourselves

And the sun
warm black-
top is a
cushion
for our
desire

*

Now I *have* kissed
your eyes, your
mouth (a hundred
times), have been
within & without
you (nakedly
disarmed
& open
to you)

Have fallen all
the way inside
you, world
you give
back to
me

Found there in-
visible threads
connect & tie
around us like a
sacred shroud,
wafer of air,
world of light-
ness, waves
from identical
currents—
karmic air

*

I cannot believe
this miracle is
happening
till you tell
me yes it
is, & then
it is, &
does …

Bellingham, Kitsilano,
Seattle, Phoenix, Alaska,
Victoria, Florida, Tuscon,
Tofino, Colorado

—it doesn't matter
where, only who
& with whom
& why

And the answers
are all there
staring us in
the face,
beckon us stop
fretting this
place (which
doesn't even
exist at
all)

*

How can you do
this, say he is
the love of
your ....
& each before
you liar,

fraud, bull
shit
dam-
aged
woman

He can only hold
what you say
in his gut
whether it
soothes or
scorches

He will choose
trust after all,
be saved from
himself after
all, like-
wise as
well

*

We're going to
end up together
(cheek to cheek)

And our lives are
going to (finally)
make some
kind of
damn-
assed
sense

It is "written"
somewhere

Let's say it
(call it)
right
here

Butts on
solid
ground

*

I swear your
spirit is in
(progressive)
flight

It flies around
& thru me
(& all the
world)

It is in constant
motion & lands
minutely in
my heart

That is each
minute's
progress,
pilgrim
that you
make of
me
(each
hour
in our
journey
here)

*

No, it cannot
end, it has
only just
begun

And it has been
waiting double
lifetimes
to take
flight

If it were to
end, life
would go
down with
it in burnt
out flames,
like it never
got off the
goddamn
soggy
ground

Life would
kill to make
this fly

It will win
or die, it
will smack
wet sky
flash
light-
ning

That goddamn
sky won't
close its
eye

Peace Eye was
supposed to be
its name way
back when

Make it so
again

*

for Katie
(intensely now)

Your spirit surely flies

What it knows

Sacred—
rimes with
your name

And true
(to me)

How could
this be?

Astonish
me, end-
lessly

(Rimes ...)

*

You worry, you
worry about me

Will she dis-
combobulate
me? Will
she put
me in
turmoil
(once again)

No— you have
taken me too
far away
stuff of
multi-
verse

Your worry
gnaws at me
(pit of my
stomach)
I cannot
live with it,
hurting you,
nor you live
properly ...

We are profoundly
connected now
(we both
know it)
& the past is
simply blown
away

Quick & vast as
the cosmos at
its start

Power enough
a lifetime
bang

Two
(even)

*

Oh lord, the deeper
you fall, the *easier*
it goes

Connection there &
you want each
other more
(one hopes)

What could be
simpler—
except the
fall itself .

But falling is
never simple,
I said, it
involves risk
& bruising
in all the
wrong
places
—like tripping
(or tripping
out)

What is this
place ? And
what are
the right
places ?

They don't teach
tender buttons in
military schools
(& all schools
are military
ones)

Drill me, you
say   —ok, I
think I can
do that
(maybe)

(Maybe you
didn't say
that ...?)

And show you
love at the
same time
(its full
range of
warm
& cool
buttons)

Let's bomb them
(the military
schools
        —on the
instalment plan)
Time-bomb &
get out of
town

All they
deserve

And I still
love you
darlin'

After all the
flashing's
gone from
the sky

And it's
darker
than any
rocket
could
remember
or show

Or shower
—like lit up
falling
rain that
cleanses
every-
thing
in its
place

*

I reach for you
… in Minnesota

Tomorrow Texas &
then Kentucky,
Tennessee

Before that
Michigan, &
later, Florida

In between we'll
be together in
two countries
(our own)

Holding each
other

Breathing …

Like we've
been some-
where

A town called
love

And it's
still in
the pink,
besides

I text a
quiet
note of
love
in the
nite

For when
yr cell is
back on
morning

Fly to me here
A-muricano woman
Power of one
hundred winged
horses on the
mesa

To me here
in the air
Neither my
city nor
yours
(nor a dalliance,
since we are
free of such
idols & idle
things!)

Where shall we
find a place
to breathe
in light
(another
question)

Here, there,
everywhere
(does it
matter?)

On the mesa
on the mountain
by the desert
by the sea

We have lived
such contrary
places

Doesn't mean
that much
to me

Lightness that
will not
fall
(fail)

*

Oh... my... god
(OMG, he sd)
isn't it time
for her sweet
strong voice
to enter... ?

Love... I have
been on a rest-
less journey.
Looking for home
that never existed.
When I look into
your eyes, I
realize I am
home. A place of
unconditional
love and
peace.

When I (too) look
in your eyes
I swear
this clenched
soul opens
right up
to receive
you
(all of you)

It is miracle
& generosity
enough

The heart thanks
you (also) for
coming home,
& soul's finger
flicks open
a long shut
door

It is not too
late, will not
slam shut in
this life-
time

Praise also the
graces & every-
thing beyond
us never
likely under-
stood by
us
trapped
against
time

Let it hand on
to us what it
will give us
as it passes
thru us
leaving traces
only of its
breath & its
breathing

*

It *is* unconditional
love, it doesn't
bounce, it
doesn't bite back,
it will never
give up or
call time on
anything
besides

And it yearns (also)
for peace & for
any remaining
peacefulness
with us especially
in tow on the
waves of its
flowing

It sits in the light-
ness of air with
two for choice,
or none
at all

It gambles reck-
lessly & is
assured of
flying
home

*

We will drive this
thing to the ends
of the earth
(or some such
frantic
cliché)

Phoenix, Portland, Ana-
cortes, Victoria,
Vancouver
—not ends of
the earth
after all (?)

Then Florida too,
so ends of this
continent
at least
(least we
can do)

My country & yours
with a knot tied
between

Invisible threads

Sutures for
the heart

Openings for
the soul

This car
drives
itself

*

They both called
him "love"
(on the daily
road)

With you, love,
it comes with
a soft Florida
purr

With her it came
with a clipped
North Ireland
heel

Jackboot &
sneakers,
love

Heel &
sole

Fleet love yet
slow right
up to the
waking
soul

*

He is awake &
he is asleep
(drowsing)
inside your
open heart

The road is
quiet, traffic
gone soft
(like the
tarmac
a while
ago)

It is an
adventure,
the buzz &
the silence
that follows
like brakes
on long
grieving
(he also
didn't
forget)

It speaks to
us in a
wishful
language
we have
not heard
before

It is road
hard
but it sees
a detour
ahead

Whispers
rest your
godawful
weary heads,
you may
have arrived
at last …

*

He thinks of you
constantly now

The unconscionable
hurt she caused
no longer even
exists

This is generosity
enough, he
wanted to
say

No, it is far
more than
that

Call it karma
(if you wish)

He thinks of you
constantly

—as miracle

Didn't 'save'
his life

Gave it 'back'
to him

Allowed its
passage
thru a
cleared
heart

*

Ok, this heart is
clear, he must
think of yours

What does it
need, where
can it go
from here,
fuel its
flight?

How can it
be free of
him?

He needs it
to soar
—otherwise it
isn't yours
anymore

And he needs
to love what
makes your
flight fuel
skies

It is an interesting
& profound
conundrum

It goes to the
pointy heart
where Zen &
existentialist
masters bow
& shake
hands

And up to the
point where
they fall
away

But that is
their problem

This conundrum
is delightfully
ours

Forever ...?

*

What's so simply
different from
before is I
believe
in you

Look in your eyes
in the dark, look
in the picture
frame beside
where I
sleep
        — I said
I *believe*
in you

When the rubber meets
proverbial road
where jet wheels
hit tarmac—
arrival gates
open to
belief in
you

Where Pacific North-
west is our half-
way house
(Phoenix &
Vancouver)
he keeps
relearning
to believe
in you

*

His parents programmed
him to cash out with
nothing less than
a woman of true
blue 'character'
(& not necessary
Tory blue, ha)

And a full face

(Proved a bit tricky
—for all at the long
table, huh?)

It has taken a
lifetime & a
miracle
(two fully
paired hands)

Bruised Jacks
& Queens
but expectations
met (despite …)

And Aces forever
gambolling in grass

What's *wrong* (?)
with this program?

Destiny has (not so)
merely trumped
human will
(more Aces)

You catch a ride
if you're lucky
& if you're
ready

And goddamn you
forever if you
don't

That goes down
the table too
(& *at* table)

                        *

We fuss for the time
we can 'come home'
to each other
every day

It's a strategy
dictated by
innumerable
things, family,
job, geography
(big one) &, of
course,
citizenship
(comrade)

We need strength
for this fretwork
& paperwork
(you have it)
& faith
            —that's
my job & I
don't have your
A-muricano
character
(I fake it)

I can only wrestle
demons to the
ground every
time they
pop up,
chaotically

I'm quick hammering
playground
things
          —like ground-
hog day come out
of season

I will get there if
you A-muricano
my arms

*

This was
meant
to be

You say it,
you have
said that

It feels
true
(to me)

Finito

*

Teach me how
you want to
be loved

I know the
answer
already

Peace (together)
thru the chaos
that surrounds
our lives,
presently

And then tomorrow
(& beyond)
filled like a cup
of yet more
peace

Until that becomes
our habit
            not just
for monks
drinking tea
in their own
enraptured
temples

*

I love u with
all my heart
she texts

Ohhh, also, he thinks,
low now
whisper
-ing
          —it has
that sound

The best life has
ever given him

Texts back he has
a future now,
of work to
make it so

                    *

Breathing Arizona …
you tell me the
air is jokingly
called dry
rain

But I know
it's you
I want
to breathe

Your after-shower
scent on my
towel

It *is* you

I breathe you
(with care, joy,
deliberate
intent)

Missing you now
for a brief while

Infuse you—
my face,
entire
being

Misting you
(yes ...)

In your
midst …
(I swear
though
absent)

*

The dreaded 'distance
relationship'
(thank god skype
half-rimes with
nite)

Halfway
cities
(half day
& nite)

And now plans
for real move-
ment (north)

God knows the
heart has
moved

He would breathe
back every
thing he ever
said

Would become
A-muricano
(for you)

Hot damn

Dry heat

Arizona
woman
in his
arms
for
dear
life

Might
kill him
(many
ways)

Frankly, he
don't care

Frank—
such an A-
muricano
name

Wear it proud,
manno

Speaks how he
feels for you,
desert
woman

Scaled down,
pure, ess-
ential

Arizona
Buddhist
minimalist
love

He breathes
your name
with a
sigh

＊

This is a waiting
'game', building
game, foundational
(like they say)

Patience has
future tense

Impulsiveness
quickly runs
present to
past imperfect

This will not
(this way) take
each other for
granted

Run that by me
again, he said

Yes, it will
fit for-
ever
(like your
sneakers,
love)

This 'game'
is deadly
serious
(that marathon
again)

Being the
last one
alive
(cross that
line)

Do not
forget
this
     —it
is a test &
it is real

Nothing else has been
(that's for sure,
old sock, old
shoe?)

Buddhist illusion?

They lose & win
together

Thinking different
things ...

That's the fundamental
beauty of what
ran by just a
moment
ago

*

Breathe life into me

You do so every single day

He has never been
so alive till now

You are here,
& you are
distant

The distance
is now
truly
close

Like a
heart
beat

*

This is a difficult
stretch, four days
makes a month
(Florida in
between)

Working damned
hard, both sides
(continental drift)

No negative
billing pls

Don't cosy up
to the sound of
don't see any
logical reason
not to …

No, pls …

No double
negatives
(prunes …)

Life is too
sweet with-
out them

                    *

We're temporarily
stuck in the gulags
here
        —couple a' zeks!

Sign on the wall says
Your patience is appreciated

Then a note flies
in thru the bars—

You are so loving.
Our paths will never
end without each
other.

Virtual road-paving
crew, linking two
guu-laags

Putting down tarmac?

Next to "Arrivals"?

(Yes, mercy pls …?)

*

Does she have
any idea
(I mean …
really?)

Must do
by now …

The heart has
been fattened

She has fed it

Feasts back
on her

Like a calf's
heart, lost,
wandering

On tarmac

Dopey, milk
fed

Sometimes
incapable
of clear
thought

Always in-
capable of
getting out
the way,
in-coming
aircraft

Help it grow
louder,
steer it

—to "Arrivals"

*

The heart gets
noisier by the
day

Pieces break
off, go
missing

Refuse to
stay silent

Wander, day-
dreamy (ropey-
dopey)

Crash into
walls

Bounce blocks
away

Call her 'home'
go running
there

Thoughtless
& alive

Home is
where …

Indeed
(thicko,
duh …)

Finally—
you have
been
truly
'found
out'
(my
son)

Nite Katie, love. A
couple more pages,
plans for dinner
w/ John A, texting
my gorgeous son.
But mostly, thinking
I don't ever want
to live again w/out
the joy u bring into
my heart.

A day of errands,
'shapping' (A-
muricano
style)

More 'saccer' shirts
(for my team)
& a "ring"
(ding-a-
ling ...
shh ...)

Plead with you
next week to
take it, wear
it, honour
it (as you
may?)

On bended knee
('saccer' ham
string permit
ting, hah)
Seattle
hotel

Right off the
tarmac, out
of Arrivals
gate

God knows how
we do these
things
(WCW)

Where the leit-
motifs are
hiding

(On & off
the run-
way)

This is a serial
poem, it needs
air (constantly)

It has only
continuance
(faithfulness?)
to offer in
return

Full of air
(& light)

Is that even
possible ...?

For you, yes
—like your
'character'
offers up
lightness
even *in*
absentia

*

Yes, miss you
terribly (horr
ibly)

74

But only an
insensitive
selfish
asshole
(indeed,
tons of
male
amperage
& sparks?)
would
not see the
'character'
(& 'honour')
on display
lighting up
the sky

Flying off
(in the midst
of it all)
across this
often dark
continent
(again ...)
to 'be there'
(as we say)

For your daughter,
sister, mother,
poor hapless
brother
(compassion
pls … in this
godawful
frightful
world that
lacks so
much of
same)

When you are
there (FL), one
can surely
see you are
specifically
'there'

One is
humbled
feels like
bowing
down to
another so
blessed,
selfless

We are
not made
so finely
our dis-
mal
selves

But our eyes
open to your
light none
the less

*

Buddhist mountain-top
retreat an hour
north of here

After a spring/summer
of post-stress eager
anticipations
we can reel in,
chill, sink into
ourselves

No-one has ever
caught a bigger
fish than us
(… we,
properly)

Nature's gifts
swim along
side

Should we
eat them or
what?

*

Karma on the
tarmac

Karma in
"Arrivals"

And for god
sake don't
forget the
fish

*

Cascadia they have
forever called it
(generations)

A dream world
to some

Pieces of your
country,
pieces of
mine

Maybe a place
in our
heads?

Maybe the
destiny
that drew
us *in* this
circle

You finish
this poem
for Cascadia
—it is yours
forever
& goes
round

*

Say it again
(on paper
this time)

I would be
A-muricano
for you

Give up my
birthright
(family,
friends)

Do your
bidding

Sell my
self

Gain new
self
(no
doubt)
part of
you

Cross borders

New land will
be your gift
to me

Already be-
come so
in your
words &
answers

*

Same tarmac
arrivals
air

Either side
of border

Borderland

Cascadia

In our minds
& hearts

Each inside
the other
        —all
that counts
(finally)

Bang, found
you

Found him
found her
(after all)

All that
is after

All that
comes
after
(hah …)

*

Wisdom friend says
being alive to your
emotions you
can hurt

Thereby not 'numb'

Come thru without
bitterness, move
on, find miracle
instead

This is the karma

Protect her,
says the
wisdom
friend

*

They are currently
near four
thousand
miles
apart

Do crows fly
straighter
than other
birds?

Love, you are
with me
forever
(she said)

They each grew
up with sea-
gulls

Shore birds
call out to
each other
constantly

This is another
continuance
(across this
enormous
continent)

—the faithfulness
of true pairs
gulled or –un

And no longer
drifting

*

Tossing around plans
(visions?)

Vancouver, Bellingham,
Seattle, Portland (OR),
—even Juneau (AK)!

Cascadia
(in fact)

Phoenix, Tuscon,
Flagstaff still
somewhere
in the mix

First we need
to sustain
time (evenly)
slow it down
make it
continuous
(is all ...)

Get off the tar-
mac, clear
Arrivals

Then head
home, where-
ever the hell
that turns
out to be

Tails on fire
sure enough
—spinning
us in even
circles …

*

He's listening to
Jarrett, he's
thinking about
her (you …)

Listens frequently
thinks (likewise)
Is obsessive?
(No …)

He's writing something

Right now

Three things on
his mind
(one, plus
two)

Living such life
on the edge
of tarmac
          —gulls
calling in
the sky

Watching for
her (you …)
feel her approach
in slow, tighter
circles
          —after
an eternity

Several eternities
(many lives
in one life)

Each (all …)
simply horrible
to live with
Soon to be
gone, ahh)

Final one gained,
engaged for
flight even
(for god sake
pls ...)

Continuance
long sought,
linked up

Round band
of light

*

This continent drifts
in a vast half circle
(south-east to
north-west)

But the ring is a
full circle

Its round band flashes
light in the sun

Pls circle the tarmac
before I die
another
lifetime

Wear my life
—sign it
with love

Be engaged
with it
after
all

*

Wear my life, I'll
carry yours

We've both been
wrong before

Not unlucky
—just wrong

Remember the numbers
this time, dial
them up any
time of nite,
love

God knows we
need to make
up for lost
time

Your Buddha
knows too

It is written
(like they say)
—the faint
copy is here

Pretentious word
nowadays (every-
one's using it)—
palimpsest

It's faint, I
feint around
it (for you)

*

You scare me,
your life is
so precious
any breath
could be
your last

And the end
of me

Why even bother
with this, don't
answer, there
is none that
anyone could
give (& to
anything
besides)

Before— there
were always
bigger things
than us, what
is the key
word here?

And that is gone,
for sure,
by now

So you simply
scare me,
that is all
you *can*
do, all
that is
left to
do,
& we
live
with
that

                    *

You are a couple hours
into the red-eye
over the pole
(more grand
circles)

Shannon, Ire (lovely)
& on to frickin'
scary Nigeria
(damn job, love)
—your heart
in your mouth
& mine along
with it
(for a ride off
the tarmac)

Probably around Cal-
Gary (oh Gary)
by now   —do NOT
de-plane, do
NOT jump, love
it will not
bring us
closer

Redneck Canuck boors,
Gary would not
catch you
(nor Cal)
just lift your
wallet &
pour

*

Poor me, poor you

Now on separate
continents
for a week
(in fact you're
on two)

I'm on first,
no, I'm at
bat

Hitting lead-
off, the scores
are minus
(minus - minus)

WTF, baseball?!
—no spice
here, no
spicer boys

Not my sport
(Sport ...)

You call mine
"saccer"
& that'll
do just
fine

*

Plenty of time for
tossing around
        —disturbed
by old dreams

He wants refuge
alongside her
(& slumbers
beside)

Can't have it
yet, she's on
a far older
continent
than he

These dreams
are beginning
to haunt,
how long can
he hold out?

Turbulent air
(in the mix)

Disturbing
nites alright,
& a nasty
palimpsest
after-taste
to their en-
cumbering
days &
ways

*

Bummed out
by a long
distance
affair

95

Bummer

Beamer (no,
only for plastik
business types
& their tykes,
or sec'taries
on weak-
ends)

Drive me to
civilization, pls

And where was
that located at,
anyway?

                    *

No worries, she
will be home
soon (& into
your heart)

Hang on, then,
gut it out
you can
do it
m-a-a-a-n

Drive her to
the town called
pink
        —in your
über-class
ice blue
get-a-way
mini-
car

                    *

She will be a star

But she will not fall
from the sky

Safe on tarmac
(my dear)

Not on the shooting
end, on the
receiving …
(open arms)

It will all be
good, &
everyone
will be
happy
after
all

He will be
zoned out …
on her
stunning
eyes &
smile

They will be
a handful
of delight,
his hands
cup her face
like a vase
made of
silk &
a single dark
& lovely
Arizona
desert
flower

*

.

No poison thoughts, pls
(your sake or his)

He is done with her (*long* ago)
& his heart is filled
with yours

If a poison thought is
furthermore untrue
it can surely bleed
more poison still

Let this one go deeply
loved woman

It has no passage left
to snake its way, a
shrivelling slithering
evil crawling thing

He also knows what
poison can do, he's
tasted it straight-
up, neat to
the tongue

Tell you a deep "buried"
secret—
he was sorely plagued
right from the get-go
the trouble thought
she came to him
slutted (not
slated) for
salvation
(ok, that's blunt)

That is why he is
done with her
(left only to
despise her
lies)

The concussed, post-
trauma, does *not* love
the concussor

You come to his heart
no red flags lying any-
where on the field

Why poison two hearts
meant to be home
each to the
other?

One is "done" when
one can no longer
respect (he's
done with her)

What more can he say?

There are so many
secret things he's
already said to *you*
he never said to
anyone before,
so many pieces
of his heart
left open
at your door

You simply *own*
his heart, by now,
desert woman, &
it is *clean* from
all poison

*

One last whack
at the tarmac
& *everything*
could change
(or not, of
course …)

It will be up to
her, the woman
should get
to choose
which ball
to hit

Choose wrong
he fades away
("not fade a-
way ...")
choose right
she makes
his day—
home-plate
(... since
his children
borne to him,
spoons in
mouth)

Spurn him madly,
he has long history
of survival,
walk bases right
outta da park

Hit tarmac too
hard, concussed
for life—
there's *nothing*
left for him

Flight-kill
on tarmac

Survival
emptied
of fuel

Caput,
Sport ...

Love done in
in the worst
horrific
late play
of his game
(& hers)

*

Clearer still —
if the terror
happened upon her,
no matter how
many adored
children, loved
friends, books
in him left to
write, he
would be
done

There's been,
already, a
lifetime of
bull-shit
horror
& lies

*

Of course the choice
has got to be yours

If you say "not really"
I'll buy you a one-
way ticket to
Phoenix

No more breathing
Arizona, that one
got choked

*

Breathing Arizona
breathing Arizona …

I promised not
to worry, flights
just go awry

Thought you'd be
in NYC last nite
(after Nigeria,
Morocco, Paris)
—stupido of me

Still no phone to-
day, no laptop, no
text connection

Slept last nite w/
the phone ready
by my pillow

Keeping my promise
to you, even w/out
pillow talk (hah!)

Breathing the twin
pillow where your
head last lay

Breathing the grace
of your head

*

Close woman friend
laughs "if she says
no, consider it a
lucky escape
... after months
of bliss"

Yup, I acknowledge,
before that they all
said "yes" & look
how far south
that went
              (past
Arizona)

Fun, huh?

Fun, fun, fun
till her daddy
took the T-
bird â-way

Do *not* flip
the bird at
me (pls,
love)

I would go south
my frickin' self

I would go alone
from now on

I would be a
lone gull
in the sky

Flapping around
off the tarmac,
staying clear of
Arrivals for
the life of
me

*

For the life of me
for the life of me ...

What does that mean?

I live in a post-
theology, post-
liturgy world

Live in fear

And (quasi-) envy
of your
Buddha

Do not re-
incarnate me

I would be
a gull, or
nothing

I do not
believe in
the Buddhas,
will that be
a problem
for you,
love?

I am a west-
coast gull,
& I fear
everything
imaginable
(& all ways)

Including
you ...?

I have no
saviour, no
origins
in sin

Only fear,
habit of
a life-
time,
love

Spare me
any curtness
(& feel no
need of
courtesy)

Give me your
love, while
it lasts
(forever …)

*

Maybe it comes right
in the end, maybe
it *will* come right
at the stop
(heart's door, valve,
wing-nut …?)

Excuse me, every-
one, for being
solipsistic,
tumescent
(& fuck you
for noticing)

Maybe it doesn't
(& up yours for
caring …
or not)

All y'all's smack
you'selves,
y'hear?

She says she'll
be the first to
offer no bullshit
psycho lies

Won't drink
what little's
left

Let's see

There is beauty
in this world
when we find it

The music a few
make, not the
crap most
'listen' to
(instantly)

And, occasionally,
in the words any
of us speaks

Words that don't
suck us dry
(she promises
me)

                            *

It is *yes*, &
we go forth
from here

We go forth
we go forth

For the life of me

Breathing Arizona

We go forth
All there is,
needs to be

And even 'need'
doesn't get
a vote, isn't
on this map

Doesn't make
fourth place,
only the two
of us, love

And no third,
either

*

Taking a nap
on the tarmac

Waiting for your
ship to come in
(on wings)

That's what he
told you he
was doing

Research for
a poem
—research
for your
touching down
(touch him, pls,
& yes again)

One in the sky
one on the ground

Making connection
every time,
kinda gulled
(at long god-
awful last,
do *not* be
fooled …)

There *are* only
the two of
us here
after
all

*

Only the two of us
(only the two of us)
what else could
there be?

All else has
failed us
(somehow)

Drowned out

We aren't complaining,
lived too long
at sea for that

Know what we
have, know
what little is
ever on offer,
on board, any-
one else
(eventually)

Know how
grateful to
look out of
our eyes w/out
unbridled fear
breaking out
(half-mast,
huh?)
freak-out city,
half-mastered
in the end

Full of promise
full of dread

This will be
ocean's roll,
not the final
drain

We have the
chance to live
again

*

She asks if he might
have second thoughts

Do not doubt her
forthright intention

Tell her instead
these are simply
last thoughts,
there is no-
thing beyond
them
(out at sea)

Only the two of us

Breathing Arizona

For the life of us

Going forth,
nothing (&
everything)
left behind
in waves of
past intent
lost at sea

*

What is there to
do, it never
gets done

Life is the same
no matter how
many times
you live
through it

What is *there*,
hiding in the
darkness?

We go forth
& the darkness
follows us

It loves us
more than
we love
ourselves,
it frames
us

We go from
grief to joy
to despair
in a click
of the shutter

The darkness
of the camera
staring at us,
blindly

*

He wants you to kill
the past, kick it
to death, bury
it in its own
awful blind-
ness

He wants to
ask you, &
doesn't know
how

He wants you to
stuff cold air
where it can
no longer
breathe

Doesn't know how
to ask you to
choke things

It seems un-
gracious,
an empty
request

Ignore it,
pls, for
your sake

*

You are beautiful
to me (that old
song)

Let's go forth …

Breathe Arizona …

No more choking

He didn't ask
you, anyway

Didn't know how

Slipped his mind

You occupy
that, truly

Occupy, what
word is
that?

It is fullness,
light in the
darkness?

Broken camera

Sudden exposure

Click, & you're
on—smile,
love

*

Breathing Arizona

Filtering the camera

Knocking the lights
out of darkness

Looking for shade

Look for each
other (in
shadow)

Know what we
have lost
& found

Don't drop
the camera,
it takes the
final pictures,
love

Say cheese
before you
drop

And mean it
(for god sake)

Drop on top of me,
I will hold you
(forever)

Don't care if
it kills me,
I have died
plenty before

I will still
hold you,
like a bird

In my gulled
hands

This is *not*
a camera,
will not
drop you

The gull
is strong
as child-
hood

It sat there on
the windowsill

Unrepentent,
ungulled
by any-
thing
at all

*

Let's fly to
Arizona,
breathe dry
rain

The forecast
is bleak
tonite
(it seems)
but clearing
tomorrow?

I'll wager
you that,
he said

With a certain,
somewhat,
confidence

That confidence
man, can
you trust
him?

Yes, pls,
you can
(& do)

This is good,
surely
(at last)

*

Do not despair,
you will hold
each other
again

The birds will
fly, the desert
blossom
(despite dry
rain)

Say it will
& he will
believe you

Go forth,
gulled to
the very
bone

It is a light bone
flies thru any
darkness
one can
throw
at it

So throw away,
shutter your
light, be
defiant in
this night
that lacks
defiance

*

On looking through correspondence
from the chilled, frozen, godawful
recent past ("the other woman")
his desert Love says to him …

… *call things not as if they were. Her emails you read were a*
blessing. You have realized you are not in bondage anymore.
Your life will be bigger and better than you ever imagined.
Do not let this snake continue her venomous sting.

His Buddha desert love
is on the mark, on the
wing again in matters
of this shoreline gull's
scavenger heart

And blessings from
her wisdom touch
pls receive with
open grace

They fly in waves
of air, dust
astonishment
across his once
crushed
face

Healing power
starts with
breathing
love

*

Breathing Arizona

Back on track,
her wisdom wings
support this
clueless gull

Lift him &
go forth

For the life of them

For the life of things
in their own
astonishment

For the life of any
thing in its own
bewildered &
slow-moving
astonishment

Bewildered, yes,
be wild of
heart &
go forth

Another grace yet
to be learned
as wings
keep time

*

More wisdom yet
from this flying
Buddha love ...

Do not read, think or
pray your way
out of such be
wilder'd spiritual
crisis, love

Look only
within

This is also where
the poems are
(he adds)
          yet they
at least hold
markers in their
(trembling) hands

You ask me this
most difficult
horror-driven
thing

How to navigate
its difficult
& discordant
music

How to be
without you
after life
closes out
(that is
another
terror,
surely)

*

She makes detailed
future plans (which
include him)

Logistics & hearts
map together
(palimpsest
again)

There is logic here
to make his heart
sing

A band of light-
flash on the
white gold
ring

*

They're throwing
curve balls at you
per day

So step out of the
batter's box
A-muricano
love
        —or hang in
there for the
slow soft one
from way deep
over here

Knock it for a
grand slam
—going for
Home

*

Going for home

Going forth

For the life of us

It is *here*,
love

Breathing Arizona

Breathing you
(breathing you,
for god sake)

Making up for
lost time
(finally)

*

This is journey's end,
stage one
(stage coach
Arizona)

And maybe finally
(full of hope,
god sake)
true beginning

... one can *believe* in

Believe in him,
you, who,
going forth,
holds his
faith

And is held
by him &
is his faith
in equal
turn

About the Author

Stephen Bett has had fifteen books of poetry published: *Breathing Arizona A Journal* (Ekstasis Editions, 2014); *Penny-Ante Poems* (Ekstasis Editions, 2013); *Sound Off: a book of jazz* (Thistledown Press, 2013); *Re-Positioning* (Ekstasis Editions, 2011); *Track This: a book of relationship* (BlazeVOX Books, Buffalo, N.Y., 2010); *SPLIT* (Ekstasis Editions, 2009); *Extreme Positions: the soft-porn industry Exposed* (Spuyten Duyvil Books, NYC, 2009); *Sass 'n Pass* (Ekstasis Editions, 2008); *Three Women* (Ekstasis Editions, 2006); *Nota Bene Poems: A Journey* (Ekstasis Editions, 2005); *Trader Poets* (Frog Hollow Press, 2003); *High-Maintenance* (Ekstasis Editions, 2003); *High Design Refit* (Greenboathouse Books, 2002); *Cruise Control* (Ekstasis Editions, 1996); *Lucy Kent and other poems* (Longspoon Press, 1983).

A sixteenth book (a selected poems) is forthcoming from Salmon Poetry, in Ireland: *The Gross & Fine Geography: New & Selected Poems.*

His work has also appeared in well over 100 literary journals in Canada, the U.S., England, Australia, New Zealand, and Finland, as well as in three anthologies, and on radio.

His "personal papers" have been purchased by the Simon Fraser University Library, and are, on an ongoing basis, being archived in their "Contemporary Literature Collection" for current and future scholarly interest.

Reviews of his books can be found at www.stephenbett.com. He lives in Vancouver.